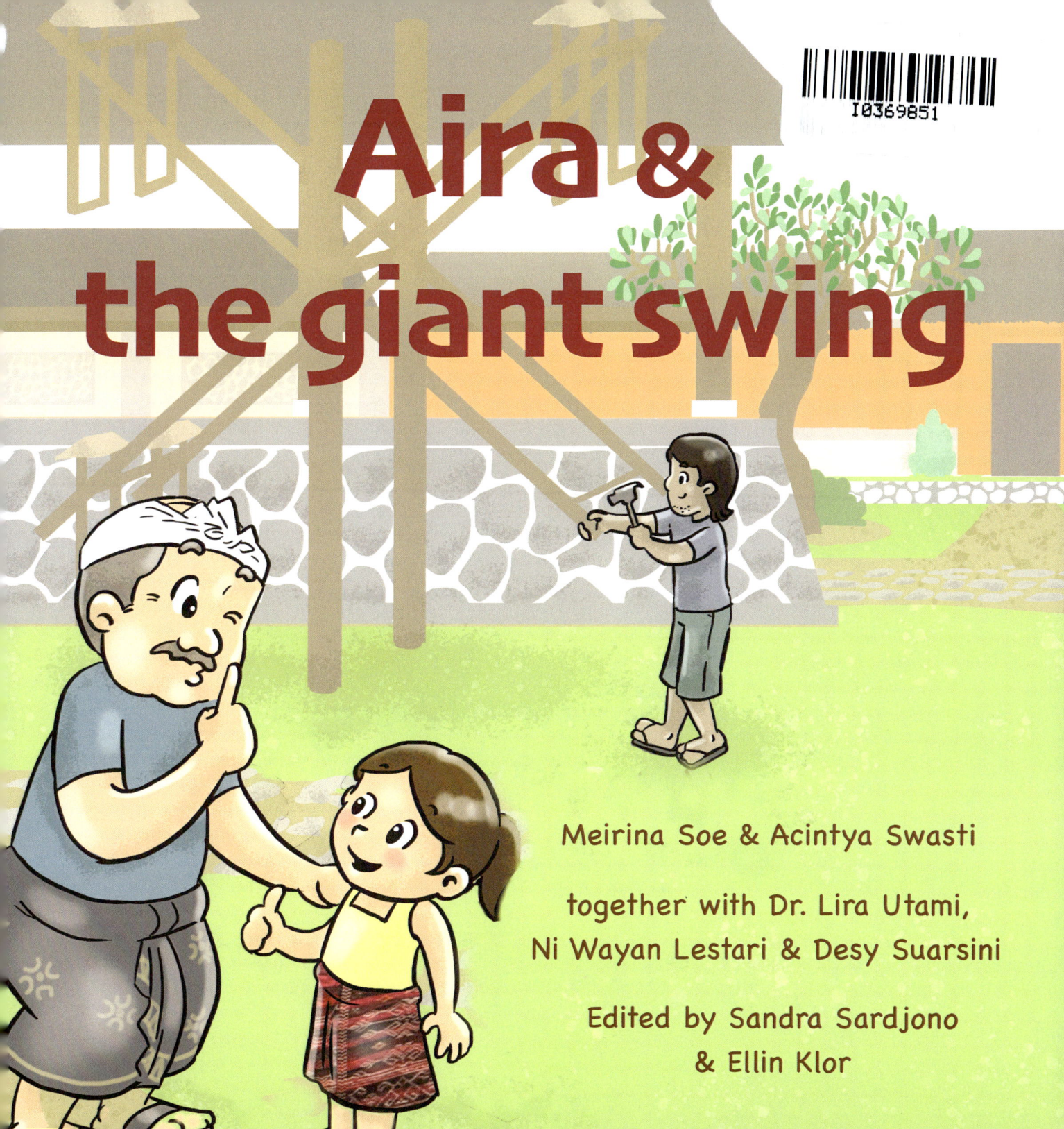

Aira & the giant swing

Meirina Soe & Acintya Swasti

together with Dr. Lira Utami,
Ni Wayan Lestari & Desy Suarsini

Edited by Sandra Sardjono
& Ellin Klor

Author: Meirina Soe,
a writer based in Surabaya, Indonesia, who has a special liking for fantasy.

Illustrator: Acintya Swasti,
an artist based in Jakarta, who has a passion for children's book.

Researcher & Story Adviser: Dr. Lira Utami,
a founding member of Design Culture Lab and a lecturer in visual communication design
at Telkom University, Bandung, with a strong passion for traditional textiles and their rich narratives.

Cultural Adviser: Ni Wayan Lestari and Desy Suarsini,
weavers in the Tenganan village, Bali.

Editor: Dr. Sandra Sardjono,
founder and president of the Tracing Patterns Foundation.

Editor: Ellin Klor,
a children's and family literacy librarian who loves textiles, reading books
and telling stories to children.

Special Acknowledgment
This book would not have been possible without support from Lira Utami, Ni Wayan Lestari and Desy
Suar who generously shared their knowledge of geringsing textile production.

Copyright © 2023 by Tracing Patterns Foundation, Berkeley, California
Produced in collaboration with Design Culture Lab, Bandung

All rights reserved. For information about permission to reproduce
selections from this book, contact tracingpatterns.org.

ISBN 978-1-7367774-8-0

On the island of Bali, there is a beautiful village named Tenganan. People say it has been there for more than 1000 years!

Women in Tenganan are experts at weaving a special cloth called geringsing *ikat*. This *ikat* cloth is worn by people during prayers in temples, as well as for special occasions such as weddings and festivals.

One of the great festivals in Tenganan is Usaba Sambah. It is a ceremony for young boys and girls when they reach a certain age.

In this village, there is a little girl named Ni Wayan Aira. And this is her story...

One sunny day, Aira was walking home from school with her father. Near the forest, they came across a giant tree wrapped in a black-and-white fabric.

"Bape, look! That tree is wearing clothes!" said Aira.

Father nodded. "Yes, dear. That tree has lived for hundreds of years. The cloth is its special robe to remind everyone to treat it kindly. It helps keep away bad luck," he explained.

Shortly after, they met two men carrying a long tree trunk.

"What is the wood for?" Aira asked curiously.

"We are building a new swing for the Usaba Sambah festival next month," one of them replied.

"I love festivals!" Aira thought excitedly. She could not wait to share this news with her sister.

Back in the village, Aira found her sister with her friends from the village girls' club, Subak Daha.

"Mbok, have you heard that the Usaba Sambah festival is coming?" Aira shouted.

"Of course!" Sister said with a big grin. "All the girls in our club have been invited to ride the giant swing."

"Oh, can I join you?" Aira asked.

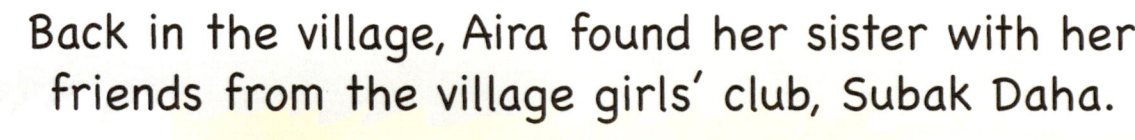

Bibi Ida is a master weaver. She enjoys teaching people, especially young girls who will carry on the tradition.

"The first rule in making a geringsing is to be patient," she said. "Remember, it's not only about the end result. You must also enjoy the process of creating it."

Bibi Ida taught Sister how to create a pattern by tying bundles of threads that are stretched on a frame.

Aira watched closely as Mbok's fingers swiftly tie knot after knot, row after row. Soon, the entire frame is filled with patterned knots.

Aira waited her turn patiently.
She was very disappointed when Bibi Ida gave
her a string of loose threads to play with.

"Bibi, please let me tie the knots like Mbok," she pleaded.

"I am sorry, my dear, Bibi Ida replied gently. "These knots require a lot of strength to tie tightly. You can help me make these knots when you are older."

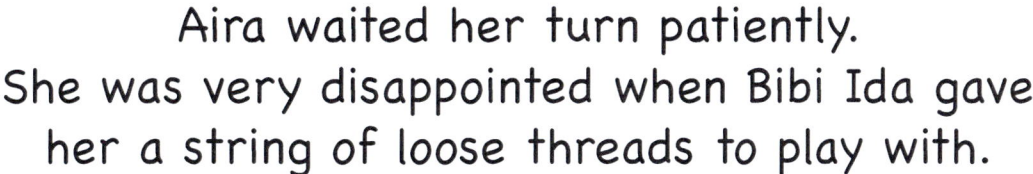

The next day, Aira accompanied her mother to the nearby Bug Bug village.

She held a box of threads that were ready to be dyed.

In the Bug Bug village, Aira saw several women dipping bundles of white threads into a large pot. When they pulled out the threads, their colors slowly changed to dark blue.

"What makes them blue?" Aira asked one of the women.

"The color comes from these leaves," said the woman, as she handed Aira a branch of indigo leaves.

Excitedly, Aira showed the leaves to her mother.

"Meme', can I bring these leaves home to dye some threads? It will be so much fun!"

But Mother disagreed. "No Aira, we cannot do that."

"Blue dyeing is not allowed in our village."

"Why?" Aira asked.

"Because this is our tradition. Blue dyeing has always been done in the Bug Bug village," Mother replied.

Some days later, Aira saw Sister and Mother working together to do the red dyeing.

Aira sat down quietly and watched.

First, Sister cut off some of the ties on the blue threads with a knife.

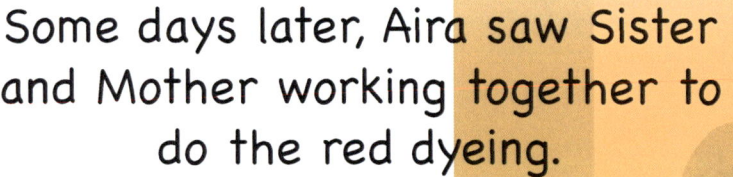

Then, Mother dipped the threads into a red dye pot. Like magic, they transformed into a vibrant red color.

"Mbok, Meme', I want to help too!" Aira pleaded.

"It's not a good idea," Mother disapproved.

"You might hurt yourself with the knife. And you're not strong enough to dye the threads evenly."

"Why don't you go and visit your grandparents?" she suggested.

Feeling unwanted, Aira went straight to her grandparents' house. She cried, "Tua, Kaki, I don't like being small. Nobody wants my help. I cannot do anything useful."

Grandmother gave her a big hug and stroked her hair. "Oh, my dear, being your age is an adventure in itself!"

"There are so many things that you can do. Come outside, and I will show you!"

"See that tall Cicempaka tree full of white flowers? Can you help me pick those flowers, Aira? I need lots of them for the offerings at the temples."

Aira was very happy that she could help Grandmother. She used a long stick to pluck the fresh flowers from the tree, one by one. She did not stop until Grandmother had collected a basketful.

The next day, Grandmother prepared another special task for Aira. She took her to the backyard, where cotton trees were in bloom.

Grandmother smiled and asked, "Can you help me pick those cotton balls? I need them to make new threads for the geringsing cloth."

Aira thought that the fluffy white cottons balls were beautiful, like little clouds.

She was very excited by this new task.

But the fun did not stop there! Grandmother introduced Aira to an intriguing machine for cleaning the cotton. It is called a cotton gin.

Aira pushed the cotton balls from one side of the machine and turned its handle. The machine worked its wonders, separating the fibers from the seeds.

Aira continued until all the cotton balls are free from the seeds, which made them even softer and fluffier.

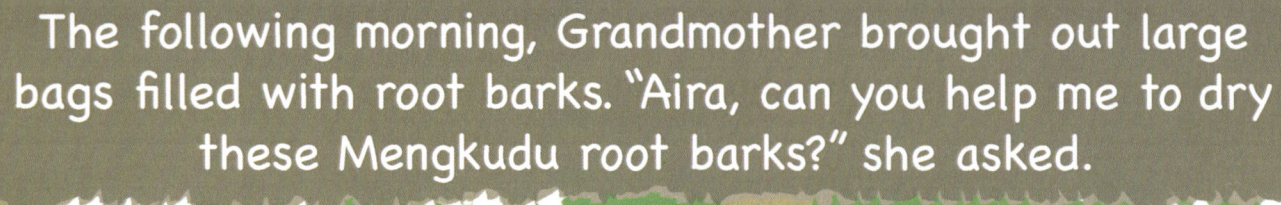

The following morning, Grandmother brought out large bags filled with root barks. "Aira, can you help me to dry these Mengkudu root barks?" she asked.

"I need them to make the red dye for the geringsing cloth."

Aira loved being Grandmother's little assistant.
She spread the root bark carefully
on a piece of cloth laid on the ground.

In the afternoon, Aira went with Grandfather to the village's main square

Aira saw several men who were making a giant swing for the festival.

During the Swing Ride, Aira's sister and the other Subak Daha girls had a great time. They screamed with joy as their seats moved back and forth and the ride spun around like a carousel.

Aira started to feel left out, but Grandfather quickly reminded her. "Remember our secret!" he said with a wink.

Right away, Aira felt better. She knew that Grandfather would keep his promise.

The boys had fun pretending to be warriors like the god Indra, who is a mighty fighter. They held a sword made of pandan leaf and a shield made of rattan.

"Go, go!" Aira cheered as the boys swiflty swung their swords.

"Whoosh!" the swords made a sound as they sliced through the air.

In the main hall, a group of girls in colorful dress performed a dance. Their hands moved slowly and gracefully, following the enchanting rhythm of the music.

Aira was completely mesmerized by the dancers. She couldn't look away throughout the entire performance.

And neither did everyone else!

The festival was also a time for prayers. Every family went to the temples to thank the gods for a good year.

They brought offerings of flowers, food, and geringsing cloth.

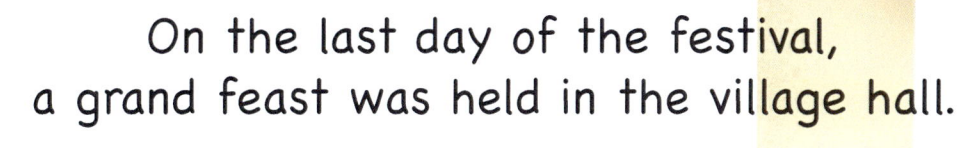

On the last day of the festival,
a grand feast was held in the village hall.

The air was filled with the fragrant aroma of food, and everything tasted incredibly delicious!

Soon, all of the festivities ended.

Aira had been waiting for this moment!

She quickly climbed onto the giant swing, and Grandfather gave it a strong push.

From above, she looked down with a big, happy smile at her grandparents.

When she reached the top, she was amazed at the view of her village and its surroundings.

Can you find these illustrations in this book of the steps to make a geringsing cloth?

1. Cleaning cotton – removing the seeds

2. Tying bundles of threads to make *ikat* patterns

3. Blue dyeing using indigo leaves

4. Taking out *ikat* ties

5. Red dyeing using mengkudu roots

6. Weaving

www.ingramcontent.com/pod-product-compliance
Lightning Source LLC
Chambersburg PA
CBRC090903080526
44587CB00008B/178